SMART GIRLS

HEALTH AND FITNESS

Style Secrets for Girls

STEPHANIE TURNBULL

W
FRANKLIN WATTS
LONDON • SYDNEY

An Appleseed Editions book

First published in 2014 by Franklin Watts
338 Euston Road, London NW1 3BH

Franklin Watts Australia
Hachette Children's Books
Level 17/207 Kent St, Sydney, NSW 2000

© 2013 Appleseed Editions

Created by Appleseed Editions Ltd,
Well House, Friars Hill, Guestling,
East Sussex TN35 4ET

Designed and illustrated by Guy Callaby
Edited by Mary-Jane Wilkins

ISBN 978-1-4451-3186-3

Dewey Classification: 613'.04242

A CIP catalogue for this book is available from the British Library.

Picture credits
t = top, b = bottom, l = left, r = right, c = centre
title page R. Gino Santa Maria/Shutterstock; page 2t TongChuwit/Shutterstock,
b iStockphoto/Thinkstock; 3 Lasse Kristensen/Shutterstock; 4l cabania, r eurobanks/both
Shutterstock; 5l Denis Babenko, r Andre Blais/both Shutterstock, b Hemera/Thinkstock;
6t Ilya Andriyanov, c alexkatkov/both Shutterstock; 7t Rafa Irusta, l gosphotodesign, cr Luis
Santos, b Cameramannz/all Shutterstock; 8t Mihai Simonia, b Svetlana Lukienko/both
Shutterstock; 9 Tomislav Pinter/Shutterstock; 10t gosphotodesign, l Yeko Photo Studio,
b Juriah Mosin/all Shutterstock; 11t CREATISTA, r Tami Freed/both Shutterstock;
12t HLPhoto/Shutterstock; 14l CGissemann, r AISPIX by Image Source/both Shutterstock;
15 stockcreations/Shutterstock; 16t Lana K, bl & r Nitr/all Shutterstock; 17 drfelice/
Shutterstock; 18 Monkey Business Images/Shutterstock; 19 iStockphoto/Thinkstock;
20 Petunyia/Shutterstock; 21b Jacek Chabraszewski, r Chris Turner/both Shutterstock;
22 AISPIX by Image Source/ Shutterstock; 23t Yuri Arcurs, b Anatoliy Samara/both
Shutterstock; 24t Polka Dot Images/Thinkstock, c Jaimie Duplass/Shutterstock; 26t YanLev,
b samotrebizan/both Shutterstock; 27t Chamille White, b Vlue/both Shutterstock;
28t mast3r/Shutterstock, bl Jupiterimages/Thinkstock, r Vibrant Image Studio/
Shutterstock; 29t Szasz-Fabian Ilka Erika, r Netfalls - Remy Musser, b Garsya/all
Shutterstock; 30t Joerg Beuge, b Raymond Kasprzak/both Shutterstock; 31 iStockphoto/
Thinkstock; 32 Jaren Jai Wicklund/Shutterstock
Front cover: iStockphoto/Thinkstock

Printed in China

Franklin Watts is a division of Hachette Children's Books,
an Hachette UK company.
www.hachette.co.uk

Contents

Smart living

Being fit and healthy makes you feel good and look great. It involves looking after your body, eating well and getting up and about. This book is packed with tips and tricks to improve your health and fitness – and help you have fun at the same time!

Enjoy yourself

Health and fitness always go together. Leading a healthy lifestyle gives you lots of energy to exercise, while plenty of exercise keeps your body growing well and working fantastically. The key is to choose healthy foods and activities that you enjoy, so you feel like you're treating your body, not punishing it!

Body benefits

Regular exercise strengthens your heart, lungs, muscles and bones. It boosts your **immune system** to fight illness and prevent disease, and stops your body storing excess fat. Exercise can improve **digestion** and **circulation** – and helps you sleep better, too.

The more energy you use, the more you have! You'll also be alert and able to concentrate well.

Body bits and bobs

Being fit lets you bend and stretch your body more. Some people can hook their feet behind their ears!

Many of your bones won't stop growing until you're about 20.

When you exercise, your body produces chemicals called endorphins that make you feel happy.

Pssst... Hot Tip!

Look out for these tips throughout the book. They give you all kinds of extra ideas and advice for keeping fit and healthy.

Freshening up

One of the simplest but most important ways to stay healthy is to keep clean. Regular washing and basic body maintenance get rid of dirt and harmful germs that cause colds, flu, tummy bugs and other illnesses.

Hand hygiene

The most common way in which germs spread is on hands – so always wash yours before preparing or eating food, after touching animals, handling anything dirty or blowing your nose, and of course after going to the toilet. Always use soap!

A daily bath or shower is great, but hair doesn't need washing every day.

When washing, don't forget the backs of your hands...

...between your fingers...

...and your thumbs.

Splish splash

Exercise makes you hot and sweaty, so always have a shower or bath afterwards. Wash well after swimming, too, as this gets rid of pool chemicals. Dry yourself carefully so skin doesn't become chapped and sore.

Use clean towels and washcloths so you don't spread germs around.

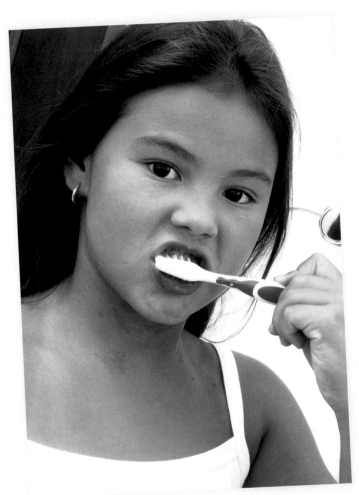

Open wide

Brushing your teeth twice a day keeps teeth and gums clean and healthy, and helps avoid bad breath, too. But don't attack your teeth with a violent burst of brushing – take at least two minutes to gently massage the brush over every tooth surface.

Pssst... Keep your bedroom clean and tidy to cut down on germs, smells and dust!

Yucky stuff

Athlete's foot is an itchy, flaky skin disease that spreads in damp places such as swimming baths.

A sneeze can send 40,000 tiny droplets of mucus spraying into the air.

Millions of germs grow under fingernails. Keep yours short and clean them with a nail brush or cotton bud.

Pamper time!

So you've got beautifully clean skin, teeth, hair and nails... now how about having some fun so you feel (and smell) completely gorgeous?

Scented soaks

If you have gift sets of bath bubbles, beads, soap or salts, make time for a really long, luxurious bath and try them out. Alternatively, add about a tablespoon of vanilla essence to your bath as you run the water to give it a delicate, delicious fragrance.

Pssst... Don't sprinkle loose herbs or flowers in your bath as you'll clog the plughole. Make a bag from a thin cotton scarf, fine net or a pair of tights.

Fresh or dried lavender gives your bath a lovely scent.

Handmade soap

To liven up plain, boring soaps, grate them into a large bowl.

Add a little water, a few drops at a time, until the mixture is soft enough to scrunch into a ball, like dough. Mix in a few drops of food colouring or perfume if you like. Mould the soap into shapes or press it into cookie cutters.

This is a good way of using leftover bits of soap.

Don't use the grater, bowl and cookie cutters for food preparation in the future.

Tea treat

You can buy **conditioner** to give your hair extra strength and shine, but it's more fun to make your own! Green tea is a simple, non-messy natural conditioner. Put two green tea bags in a jug, carefully fill with boiling water and leave for about 30 minutes to cool.

Remove the bags and pour the tea on shampooed and rinsed hair. Leave for about three minutes, then rinse off with cool water.

Don't overdo it!

Although you want to smell fantastic, remember that using too many strongly-scented lotions and perfumes can be overpowering – and they may irritate your skin. When trying new products, always test them on a small patch of skin first to check you're not **allergic** to them.

Healthy eating

Eating well is a vital part of being healthy. It helps your body grow properly and gives you strength and energy. Cuts, bruises and broken bones heal faster, skin glows and even your hair and nails look better.

Pick and mix

The secret of healthy eating is to choose a variety of foods, so your body gets a good mix of **nutrients**. Foods such as bread, pasta and rice are packed with energy-giving **carbohydrates**, while meat, fish, eggs and beans contain **protein**. You also need lots of **vitamins** and **minerals** from fruit, vegetables and dairy products.

Use your head

There's no need to diet, avoid some food altogether or obsess over food labels – just think smart! Don't eat lots of fatty or sugary things, and try to choose fresh ingredients – the less **processed** your food is, the less hidden salt, sugar and fat it's likely to contain.

A baked potato with tuna and salad makes a healthy, filling lunch.

Pssst... Eat when you feel hungry, but stop as soon as you're full.

Snack attack

Instead of snacking on chocolate bars or crisps, try mixed seeds, dried fruit or a smoothie (see page 16). They're more filling than you might think. Or why not make your own spiced popcorn? It contains no salt or sugar – unlike most pre-made popcorn.

1. Put 100g popping corn into a big pan. Cover with a well-fitting lid and heat gently, shaking every so often.

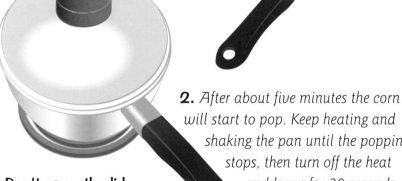

Don't open the lid while it's popping!

2. After about five minutes the corn will start to pop. Keep heating and shaking the pan until the popping stops, then turn off the heat and leave for 30 seconds.

3. In another pan, gently heat a tablespoon of olive oil and a generous sprinkle of ground spice, such as curry powder, cinnamon, Chinese five-spice or cayenne. Stir in handfuls of popcorn and toss to coat it in the mixture.

Experiment with a range of spices.

Funny food

Insects such as ants, beetles, crickets, grubs and scorpions are full of nutrients and can be eaten fried, roasted or boiled.

Some types of carrots are purple.

Durians are south-east Asian fruits that stink of sweaty socks and rotten onions – but taste delicious!

Clever cooking

Healthy meals shouldn't be boring! Find recipes in the library or online, and don't be afraid to try new or unusual foods. Remember to wash your hands first and ask for adult help, especially when using the oven.

Try couscous, a North African food made from wheat.

Roasted veggie wedges

If you find boiled vegetables bland, roast them instead – they taste delicious and are a brilliant alternative to chips.

1. Preheat the oven to 200 °C (180 °C fan oven, 400 °F, gas mark 6). Chop vegetables into bite-sized chunks. Aubergines, courgettes, butternut squash, sweet potatoes (washed but not peeled), carrots and red onions all work well.

2. Put the vegetables in a roasting tin, drizzle on a tablespoon of olive oil and turn to coat everything in oil. Cook for about 20 minutes.

Cherry tomatoes also roast well in about 10 minutes.

Pssst... Turn roasted veggies into a great pasta bake by stirring in cooked pasta and a few tablespoons of low-fat **crème fraîche**, then heating in the oven.

Soy salmon bake

This tasty dish uses salmon, which is full of protein and **omega-3 fatty acids**, which are great for your heart. It serves four, but you can adapt it for more or fewer people.

You will need:
- ♥ 4 salmon fillets
- ♥ 1 red pepper, seeds removed
- ♥ 4 spring onions, trimmed
- ♥ thumb-sized chunk of fresh ginger, peeled
- ♥ 1 carrot, peeled
- ♥ 2 tbsp soy sauce
- ♥ 1 orange, squeezed
- ♥ 250g egg noodles
- ♥ 2 tbsp sesame seeds

1. Preheat the oven to 200°C (180°C fan oven, 400°F, gas mark 6). Slice the vegetables thinly.

2. Tear four large pieces of tin foil and fold them in half. Place a salmon fillet in the middle of each and pile vegetable strips on top.

3. In a bowl, mix the soy sauce and orange juice, then pour some over each fillet. Curl up the foil so the sauce doesn't run everywhere.

4. Scrunch the foil edges together over the fillets. Place on a baking tray and cook for 15 minutes.

5. Meanwhile, cook the egg noodles in boiling water according to the packet instructions. Gently heat the sesame seeds in a frying pan until golden.

6. Drain the noodles and spoon into bowls. Lay the fillets on top, pour over any sauce from the foil and sprinkle on the sesame seeds.

Fresh coriander makes a great finishing touch.

Sweet stuff

There's no need to deny yourself dessert – just eat small portions and choose light, low-fat or reduced sugar options when you can. Even better, make your own desserts so you know exactly what is in them.

Fruity yoghurt

Fresh fruit tastes great on its own, but if you want something different, heat berries or chopped fruit such as mangoes, apples or peaches in a pan with a little water until soft. Purée them in a blender and swirl into low-fat yoghurt.

Try puréed fruit and yoghurt with granola for a healthy breakfast.

If you love ice cream, choose a small scoop in a cone rather than a big tub or bowl!

Pssst... Don't forget that canned fruit is good for you, too – as long as there is no added sugar in the juice.

14

Baked bananas

Make a quick, tasty pudding by slicing a peeled banana lengthways. Lay it on tin foil with pecans, walnuts or chopped dates and drizzle a teaspoon of honey on top. Scrunch the foil into a parcel, place on a baking tray and cook at 200°C (180°C fan oven, 400°F, gas mark 6) for 15 minutes. Leave to cool a little before eating.

Chocolate mousse

Try this for a special occasion! The secret ingredient is **tofu**, which creates a thick, creamy mixture without extra fat or sugar.

You will need:
- ♥ 200g bar dark or milk chocolate
- ♥ 340g carton silken tofu
- ♥ 2 tbsp smooth, low-sugar jam
- ♥ ½ orange, squeezed
- ♥ 1 tsp vanilla extract

1. Break the chocolate into chunks in a microwaveable bowl and heat in 20-second bursts until melted, stirring regularly so it doesn't burn. Be careful – the bowl will get hot.

2. Using a hand-held liquidizer or blender, purée the tofu until smooth and creamy. Add the jam, vanilla and 3 tablespoons of orange juice, then mix again.

Making individual portions stops you eating too much – and they look good, too!

3. Add the melted chocolate and purée until smooth and creamy. Pour into bowls or glasses and refrigerate for at least two hours.

Drink up!

Your body needs a constant supply of water to work properly, digest food and grow. Without it you become **dehydrated**, which makes you thirsty, weak and dizzy. The best and easiest way to keep your water levels topped up is by drinking plenty of it!

Try to get into the habit of taking a small bottle of water out with you.

Feeling thirsty?

Fruit juices contain water, but make sure they don't also have added sugar. Instead of fizzy drinks, try herbal teas – they're much healthier, kinder to teeth and can help freshen your breath, too.

Pssst... On hot days, why not try freezing fruit smoothies in ice lolly moulds?

Super smoothies

Smoothies are really healthy drinks and a great way of eating lots of fruit in no time at all. They're also fun to make as you can use whatever fruits you like. Blend chopped fruit on its own or add milk and low-fat natural yoghurt for a creamy milkshake.

Lemon refresher

For a cool drink on a hot day, combine iced tea with homemade lemonade to make this sparkling mixture. It's thirst-quenching and bursting with vitamin C.

1. *Pour boiling water on a handful of fresh mint and leave for about 10 minutes.*

3. *Strain the mint tea into the glass and stir in a teaspoon of sugar.*

2. *Squeeze the juice of a lemon into a glass, removing any pips.*

4. *Chill in the fridge then top up with fizzy water.*

Alternatively, leave out the sugar and top up with diet ginger ale.

Did you know?

Energy drinks often contain caffeine, which can make you anxious, grumpy and unable to get to sleep at night.

Every day your body loses more than two litres of water, which need replacing through drinks and food.

A can of cola contains about eight teaspoons of sugar.

Start exercising

Keeping fit doesn't mean long, gruelling workouts. Just try to be active for about an hour every day (not necessarily all at once), and do lots of different activities – that way you'll benefit your whole body.

Warming up

Launching straight into energetic activities can cause injuries, so prepare your body first. Spend five minutes doing gentle exercises to loosen and warm your muscles, get **joints** moving smoothly and raise your heartbeat gradually so as not to strain your heart.

How many skips can you do before you're out of breath?

Warming up can involve marching, jogging or bouncing on the spot...

... then lifting your arms and raising your knees higher with each step...

... and finally giving each part of your body a shake and a gentle stretch.

Healthy heart

Any activity that makes your heart beat faster is called aerobic exercise. It strengthens your heart and helps it pump blood more efficiently around your body. Here's how to check your heart rate.

1. Hold out your arm, palm up. Using the first two fingers of your other hand, find the bony bit on your wrist, below your thumb. Press down lightly around it until you feel your pulse.

2. Count your pulse for a minute. It should beat between 70 and 100 times.

3. Now do ten minutes of aerobic exercise and check your heart rate again. The target to aim for is about 130 beats per minute.

60 secs

Take a deep breath...

Regular exercise strengthens your lungs so that they can hold more air and give your body extra oxygen. This helps you exercise more and grow even fitter.

To see how much air your lungs hold, stretch a balloon, take a deep breath, then – in one go – breathe out all the air into the balloon. Measure the balloon and repeat after a few weeks of exercising to see if your lungs have improved!

Don't blow so hard that you make yourself feel dizzy.

Pssst... If you're exercising with friends, warm up by throwing or kicking a ball to each other.

Super sports

What kind of exercise do you like? Perhaps you enjoy team games with friends, or maybe you prefer solo sports. If you're really not keen on sport, don't despair! Try some of these ideas – one might be perfect for you.

Pssst... Start a new sport with a close friend – you'll feel much less nervous.

Clubs and classes

Joining a sports club or class is a great way to try new things. How about combat sports such as taekwondo, or indoor climbing on artificial rock walls, or skiing on dry ski slopes? Fitness classes such as zumba for kids are great if you like to dance.

Get out and about...

Family hiking or camping trips feel more like holidays than sports, but they can be very energetic. Other fun outdoor sports include orienteering and geocaching, in which you use a **GPS receiver** or mobile phone to locate hidden prizes.

In orienteering, every time you find a marker you punch your card with the special hole punch provided.

If you find a geocache, take one of the small gifts and put a new one inside. There is also a log book to fill in.

...or stay indoors!

If going outside doesn't appeal, watch exercise videos on TV or online, or play interactive sports on games consoles. As long as they get your heart beating faster, they count as sport!

Water workout

Swimming is a great body workout, whether you go to classes, compete in races or just splash in the pool on holiday! It can also lead to other aquatic sports such as water aerobics, water polo, snorkelling, canoeing or even synchronized swimming.

Strange sports

Zorbing is a sport in which people roll along the ground in a transparent plastic ball.

Canine freestyle dancing involves dogs and their owners performing musical routines together.

Other unusual sports include stair racing, swamp football, toe wrestling and joggling (a combination of juggling and jogging).

Fun and games

Exercise doesn't have to mean playing organized sports – you can make up your own games to play with your friends. Here are some brilliant ideas for the park or garden.

Chasing games

Playing tag is a great way of getting up and about, but why not invent new rules? Perhaps people who are tagged have to lie down until someone tickles them. Or maybe everyone has to play while balancing beanbags on their heads, or carrying plastic cups of water that they mustn't spill!

Crazy courses

Get creative with a garden obstacle course! It could include doing five twirls of a hula hoop, keeping a balloon off the ground for a minute without using your hands, crawling under garden chairs, splashing through a paddling pool or pegging five items of clothing on a washing line as fast as you can!

Brave the weather

Wet and windy weather needn't stop you going outside. How about trying to catch leaves in the wind, jumping over puddles, or running as fast as you can from one shelter to another?

Super snow

There's so much to do in snow! Building snowmen, having snowball fights or pulling a sledge up a hill will get you out of breath in no time. You could also try digging a winding maze in deep snow or designing an intricate pattern of footprints.

Pssst... Don't spoil the fun by getting too competitive. It really doesn't matter who wins your made-up games!

23

No-fuss fitness

There are many ways of finding time for exercise in everyday life. Get into the habit of doing some of these activities and you'll be fitter without even realizing it.

Don't forget that a trip to the shops can count as exercise as long as you do plenty of brisk walking!

Help at home

Household chores could earn you some extra pocket money as well as improve fitness. Walking the dog, washing the car, vacuuming the house and raking leaves all burn lots of energy.

Walk and talk

Try using your legs instead of your mobile – could you walk to a friend's house with a message instead of texting from home? At the park, stroll as you chat rather than sitting on a bench. If you're busy gossiping, you'll walk miles without realizing!

Pssst... Get a **pedometer** to see how far you walk in a day. Think of ways to increase your daily total.

Amazing music

Dancing to your favourite music is a wonderful way of getting out of breath – and it can cheer you up, too. Listen to lively music on headphones when out walking, as the beat helps you keep up a brisk pace.

TV workouts

Sitting slumped in front of the TV is terrible for your posture and makes you tired and sluggish. Here are some top tips for healthier TV-watching.

1. *Sit up properly. This doesn't mean holding your back rigid – instead, pull back your head so your ears are above your shoulders. Relax shoulders and keep feet flat on the floor.*

2. *Do gentle stretches to avoid aches and stiffness. Hold out a leg and rotate your ankle, stretch both arms to the sides and circle them, or touch your shoulders and gently pull your elbows back. Do each action a few times.*

3. *Get up regularly. Make it a rule that you walk or march on the spot during ad breaks. If you're with friends, you could dance or do certain moves, such as hopping during perfume ads and star jumping during food ads!*

Stay safe

Staying fit and healthy means using your head and looking after yourself. Here are some tips for avoiding injury and illness.

Get the gear

Wear loose-fitting, comfortable cotton clothes for exercise. Take off jewellery and make sure you have trainers that don't rub. Carry an extra layer to put on after exercise, as your body goes on sweating and losing heat, leaving you shivery.

Certain sports need special safety gear – such as a hard hat for riding.

Cool down

If you do lots of exercise then stop suddenly, your muscles may become stiff and sore. Do a few gentle cooling down stretches to relax your muscles and gradually lower your heart rate.

Don't overdo it

Too much exercise is bad for you – it can strain your heart and muscles, leave you gasping for air and make you feel sick. Take it easy and stop before you're completely exhausted. Always drink plenty of water to replace the fluid your body has lost through exercise.

Pssst… Don't exercise if you're full of cold. Give your body a few days to recover.

Outdoor dangers

Think before heading out. Wear layers on cold days and a hat and sun block in warmer weather. Be aware of traffic and other people around you. Make sure an adult knows where you are, and don't go on long walks or bike rides alone. Taking a phone is also a good idea.

Wear a helmet when cycling and stay alert near traffic and pedestrians.

Watch out for...

Cramp: the painful feeling when muscles suddenly tense up. Try gently stretching and rubbing the area until it relaxes. Drinking plenty of water also helps.

Heat exhaustion: happens when your temperature rises so high that you feel sick and dizzy. Avoid it by drinking water and not exercising in extreme heat.

Indigestion: stomach pains that can be caused by exercising after eating, especially if you've had a big meal. Wait an hour or two after meals before doing vigorous exercise.

And relax...

Knowing how to wind down and relax is as important for your body as diet and exercise. But this doesn't mean vegging out in front of the TV or computer for hours – it's about being calm, controlled and composed.

Ditch the stress

To really relax, you need to clear your head. Pick a time when you won't be disturbed by anyone. Go somewhere quiet and private such as your bedroom or the garden. Sit comfortably.

Close your eyes and conjure up a relaxing image. Perhaps you're on a beach, or floating in space. Breathe slowly and imagine each part of your body relaxing in turn.

Chill out

If you're just too fidgety to sit quietly (or likely to fall asleep!) then there are many other ways to relax. Have a bath, dance, play a musical instrument, cuddle your pet, reorganize your wardrobe or look at old photo albums… Do whatever makes you feel calm and happy.

Listening to favourite music may be a perfect way to unwind after a busy day.

Pssst… Think positive! Focus on things that make you feel good about yourself, and try not to worry too much.

Be organized

Sticking to good routines makes you less likely to forget important things and then panic about them. Do homework or chores early in the day, so you're not working (or stressing) late at night. Wind down before bed by reading or writing a diary instead of watching TV, texting or staring at a computer.

1) Ask about project
2) Buy new earphones
3) Ring Beth

Making a to-do list before bedtime can help you clear your mind and fall asleep more easily.

Goodnight… zzz

Go to bed at a reasonable time; you need about nine or ten hours' sleep every night. Without this you'll be low on energy – and grumpy, too – all day. And that may tempt you to eat sugary foods for quick energy bursts.

Glossary

allergic
Extra-sensitive to something, leading to bad reactions such as sneezing and skin rashes, or sometimes even dizziness and difficulty breathing.

carbohydrates
Natural substances your body needs for energy. There are two types: starch (in foods such as bread and pasta) and sugar.

circulation
The constant flow of blood around your body, pumped by your heart.

conditioner
A creamy liquid rubbed into wet, clean hair and rinsed off to help make it shiny and smooth.

crème fraîche
A type of thick cream that doesn't taste sweet. It is often used in hot dishes because it won't separate into lumps when heated.

dehydrated
Not having enough water in your body, which means that it can't work properly.

digestion
The process of breaking down food in your body and turning it into chemicals that your body uses to grow and work properly.

GPS receiver
A device that picks up signals from satellites in space and uses them to work out its location. GPS stands for Global Positioning System.

immune system
Parts of your body that work together to destroy germs and keep you healthy.

joint
A place where two bones meet in your body.

minerals
Nutrients in food that your body needs to stay healthy. Important minerals include calcium, iron and zinc.

nutrients
Natural substances found in plants and animals that your body needs to work properly.

omega-3 fatty acids
A healthy type of fat that is found in oil from fish and some plants.

pedometer
A small electronic device, often worn on a belt, which counts every step a person takes by sensing the movement of their hips as they walk.

processed
Fresh ingredients that have been cooked, canned or frozen. Processing can make food safer by killing bacteria, but extra fat, salt or sugar is sometimes added, for example in ready meals and cereal.

protein
A substance found in many foods that your body needs to grow and become strong.

tofu
A food made from soya beans and water, pressed into blocks that look like white cheese. Tofu can be used in both savoury and sweet dishes.

vitamins
Natural substances in food that your body needs to work properly and grow strong.

Smart sites

www.longlocks.com/hair-care-recipes-cookbook.htm
Lots of ideas for making your own natural shampoos and conditioners.

www.kidshealth.org/kid/recipes
All kinds of imaginative recipes for tasty meals and snacks.

www.allrecipes.co.uk/recipes/tag-5685/kids-smoothie-recipes.aspx
Fun, easy ideas for creating delicious fruit smoothies.

www.nhs.uk/Change4Life/Pages/change-for-life-families.aspx
Handy hints and tips to keep you and your family active and healthy.

www.monkeysee.com/play/1494-fitness-for-kids-warm-up-routine
Short videos to help you warm up and exercise properly.

www.kidspot.com.au/kids-activities-and-games/fun-outdoor-activities-for-kids+9.htm
More than 100 suggestions for outdoor games and fun!

Index